DELI  BONDAGE OF THE SPIRIT HUSBANDS AND WIVES

(Incubus And Succubus)

By,

AUGUSTINE AYODEJI ORIGBO

Copyright © 2014 Augustine Ayodeji Origbo
All rights reserved.
ISBN: 9781499374728

DEDICATION

This work is dedicated to the ALL MIGHTY GOD, The Ancient of Days, the author and creator of life; Jehovah-Elohim.

DELIVERANCE FROM BONDAGE OF THE SPIRIT HUSBANDS AND WIVES

TABLE OF CONTENTS

ACKNOWLEDGEMENT
FORWARD.
CHAPTER ONE: Who is a spirit husband or wife?
CHAPTER TWO: Signs of the presence of the spirit husbands or wives.
CHAPTER THREE: Problems associated with having a spiritual husbands or wives.
CHAPTER FOUR: How does a spirit husband or wife access their victim's lives?
CHAPTER FIVE: Steps to dealing with the spirit husband and wife phenomenon.
CHAPTER SIX: Prayer points to demolish spiritual husband /wife.
ABOUT THE AUTHOR

DELIVERANCE FROM BONDAGE OF THE SPIRIT HUSBANDS AND WIVES

ACKNOWLEDGEMENT

There is no noteworthy achievement that can be accomplished without the collective efforts of likeminded persons. At the risk of omitting someone important; this book is a result of such synergistic association and investments of the persons listed below.

A special thanksgiving to the almighty God the creator of all things who gave the inspiration for this work. I also appreciate my biological father and mother Mr. and Mrs. Paul and Rebekah Origbo for their regular parental support.

To my best friend and wife Mrs. Marie Jeanne; thank you for your love and support.

Augustine Ayodeji Origbo

DELIVERANCE FROM BONDAGE OF THE SPIRIT HUSBANDS AND WIVES

FORWARD

The spirit wife and husband phenomenon, though not often spoken about by many, is one of the most dangerous avenues through which Satan and his demons access life's, homes and other various life institutions, to cause both physical and spiritual damages to mankind. Many today are having these experiences and instead of finding a way to deal with them, they are practically enjoying it and ignorantly suffering the consequences. They do not know that every relationship with a demonic being, either consciously or unconsciously, will lead into serious demonic possession, control and several other evil consequences. Certain experiences like life disorganization, marital unfaithfulness, divorce, late marriage, business failure, disoriented homes, demonic soul-tie, soul or spirit pollution by demonic spirit, and ministerial pitfall all have their roots in the attack or operation of spiritual husband/wife. Until you understand their mode of operation and how to avoid their evil influence in your life, you may never be able to fully fulfil your destiny here on earth. This little book is an eye-opener to the various operations of these sexual demons call incubus and succubus. It will not only open your eyes to the truth behind this spiritual phenomenon, but it will also help you to permanently destroy their stronghold and terminate their operations in your life. Stay blessed as you read.

Yours,

Augustine Ayodeji Origbo

CHAPTER ONE

WHO IS A SPIRIT HUSBAND OR WIFE?

Spirit husbands or wives are not human beings; they are demonic entities or agents of darkness sent into lives, homes or households by Satan to serve as demon husbands or wives, evil lords, evil governors, demonic manipulators, ancestral curse executors, and robbers of the glory and blessings of their victims. Spirit husbands or wives are those negative forces that appear with familiar faces in dreams to have sexual relationship or intercourse with their victims (male or female). They can appear in different forms depending on the sexual characteristics of their victim i.e. as INCUBUS (THE MALE MANIFESTED SEXUAL DEMONS) OR SUCCUBUS (FEMALE MANIFESTED SEXUAL DEMON). They can also appear in the image of one's husband or wife, admirers, past or present boyfriends or girlfriends, so as to look appealing or familiar to their victim in their dreams. The spirit husband or wife however can also take the image of an unknown but good-looking person in the dream so as to have sexual intercourse with their victims. If when you sleep, either in the day or night-time, you dream of someone you admire, such as your hero, heroine, husband or wife having sexual intercourse with you, it is not your hero, heroine, husband or wife; it is a demonic spirit using the image of those people to appear in your dream to have sex with you in order to pollute you, poison you and take some valuable spiritual substances needed for your life's effectiveness from you. The Bible stated very clearly what the devil's job is.

The thief cometh not, but for to steal, and to kill, and to destroy: I am come that they might have life, and that they might have it more abundantly (John 10:10)

Satan's job is to steal, destroy and kill. If he knows he cannot destroy or kill a person in the physical world, he will try to do so bit by bit through the spirit world i.e. through dream manipulations, demonic spiritual initiations and spirit wife or husband attacks. Sexual intercourse is not to be done in the dream. The word of God allows sexual relationship or intercourse between two people (a man and his wife) legally married in the physical and not among unmarried people, which is one of the causes of the attack of spirit husband and wife.

As marriage is only permitted in the physical world and not in the dream, likewise is sexual relation only permitted in the physical world between a husband and his wife. It is not to be done in the dream. If you had sexual intercourse with a man or a woman that looked like your spouse in the dream, to know if that person you have had sexual relationship with in the dream is your spouse or not, simply ask your spouse after waking up from such dreams if he or she saw you having sexual intercourse with him or her in the dream. You will discover that the response will be NO! If the response is no, who then is that person with the image of your husband or your wife whom you derive sexual pleasure from regularly in dreams? That person in that dream is your spirit husband, otherwise known as incubus (the male manifested sexual demon), or your spirit wife or succubus (female manifested sexual demon).

CHAPTER TWO

SIGNS OF THE PRESENCE OF SPIRIT HUSBAND OR WIFE IN A LIFE

Here are some signs that show that a person has a spirit wife or a spirit husband in his or her life. So if you notice any of these experiences in your life, then you need to understand that you have a spirit husband or wife that you seriously need to destroy out of your life.

1. Constant or irregular sexual relationship or intercourse with known or unknown persons with the

same or different faces in the dream. Sometimes the spirit husband/wife may appear physically, only to be seen by their victim, and after having sexual intercourse with their victim they will disappear again into the realm of the spirit.

2. Having sexual intercourse with an invisible being or sensing an invisible presence harassing you sexually in the dream, which often leads to strange sexual excitation, ejaculation, bleeding, unusual menstruation or bedwetting.

3. Consistent miscarriage

4. Swimming, inordinate playing or dancing with a strange man or woman in the dream

5.   Having dream of strange beings having sexual relationship together or seeing a strange being with giant male organ trying to molest or abuse you in the dream

6.   When you find yourself always getting married in the dream, with the same man or even different men, then you have a spiritual husband. The same applies to a man who finds himself getting married to the same woman or different women in the dream.

7.   Successive sexual intercourse with a strange man or woman by the seaside in the dream

8.   If you are a lady and you are having dreams of regular sexual

intercourse with your father, your brother, your girlfriend or an unknown lady, that is the work of the sexual demons, otherwise known as a spiritual husband or wife, disguising to pollute you.

9. When you see yourself getting pregnant regularly and giving birth to children in the dream, with no evidence of physical pregnancy and childbirth, you have a spiritual husband who is impregnating you in the dream world.

10. Not being able to bear children in the physical or real world but having many children in display in dreams

11. Successive business failure

12. Late marriage or no marriage at all

13. Hatred for the opposite sex. Some ladies just hate men without any reason, and likewise some men hate ladies. This is because they already have a spiritual husband or wife that satisfies them sexually and makes every other human being to be repulsive to them.

14. Strange lust or desire for sexual act without considering who is involved in the act: Some people can have sexual intercourse with anything. They don't care whether the person is good, bad, ugly, too young or too old. They can even go as far as having sexual intercourse

with animals. That is the work of the demonic injections or demonic deposits transferred into their body by spiritual husband or wife during sexual intercourse in the dream.

15. All those practicing homosexuality or lesbianism have spiritual wife/husband.

16. When you suddenly develop serious and unjustified hatred for your spouse, spiritual husband is in operation.

17. Some men or women are very good at telling lies, and it is because they have a spiritual husband or wife who instructs them to do so.

Other signs of the presence of spirit

DELIVERANCE FROM BONDAGE OF THE SPIRIT HUSBANDS AND WIVES

husband/wife include:

18. Sudden fear

19. Chronic addiction to pornography

20. Masturbating

21. Procrastination of profitable inventions

22. Chronic hardship

23. Evil delay

24. Chronic poverty

25. Restlessness

26. Strange tumour in the reproductive organ of the woman

27. Bedwetting

28. Strange or bad body odour

29. Loss of memory

30. Brain dullness

31. Consistent desire to hurt others

32. Divorce or constant threat of separation in marriage

33. The presence of terminal or strange diseases in the body

34. Evil or strange marks in the body during sleep or after dreaming

35. Constant depression

36. Ancestral spirit domination

37. Consistent failure

38. Abnormal trait or character manifestation

39. Strange anger

CHAPTER THREE

PROBLEMS ASSOCIATED WITH HAVING A SPIRITUAL HUSBAND OR WIFE

As I have said in the previous chapters of this book, spirit husbands or wives are demonic entities that operate mostly through sexual intercourse in dreams so as to make their victims eternally captive to the devil. Let us quickly examine some serious consequences of having a spirit husband or wife.

1. Evil spiritual control and manipulation: Sexual intercourse with any entity, either known or unknown, in the dream will automatically lead to an evil union, and an evil union on the other hand will lead to evil or demonic control and manipulations. During sexual intercourse in the dream, pleasure does take place but it will eventually establish a covenant. For instance, if you derive sexual pleasure from a demonic being who appears in the image of a man or woman you know in the dream, it means that the force behind that being you had sexual intercourse with in the dream has transmitted something into your body, which permits you to enjoy such pleasure at that time. As such pleasure is transferred into your body during such sexual act in the dream, some valuable virtues in you will be taken by the force behind that transferred pleasure. Hence, consciously or unconsciously you have shared something in common with the evil force, and this will now be used to control every activity in your life here in the physical world. When you suddenly find yourself taking wrong decisions that are putting you into serious debt, losses, quarrels and danger, it is the effect of the evil poison of evil control injected into your body through the various sexual acts you have had in the dream with a spirit husband/wife.

2. Laziness and lack of productivity:

Captives or victims of spirit husband or wife are often lazy towards taking vital decisions about their life's progress. They are good in procrastinating, and are very often confused about what direction they are to take in order to be productive. This is because of the fear emanating from the evil deposits from the spiritual husband or wife in their body. This of course often leads to unproductive life.

3. Evil covenant is strengthened: During sexual intercourse in dreams, past evil covenant made by oneself, family members or the community with demonic forces are strengthened, thereby breeding another intense control of Satan over someone's life. If you are born again and saved by the saving grace of our Lord Jesus Christ and you still haven't broken the evil covenant of the past, whether the one made by yourself, your father, mother, ancestral parents or community, with Satan, spiritual husband or wife will because of these unbroken covenants access your life through dreams to have sexual intercourse with you so that your blood\semen\sperm can be used to renew or tighten the covenants, knowing fully well that during sexual intercourse there is a shedding of a substance equivalent to blood or life.

4. Regression and rejection will set

in. Having sexual intercourse in the dream will lead to constant failure, rejection and regression in life. Many are suffering some unexplainable rejection everywhere they turn to for help because of this. Irrespective of how good-looking and qualified they are, because spiritual husbands or wives during sexual intercourse in the dream usually spread their evil odour on their victims to make them suffer constant rejection before men. The victim will just become an object of rejection and a transporter of demonic odours. If you are a man or a woman and you have had sexual intercourse with a woman or a man who has a spiritual husband/wife, you are likely going to contact this evil odour of rejection that can make you become a rejected fellow in the society. Strange sickness and invisible chains may have also have been put upon your life. You will need to quickly deliver yourself by praying your way into deliverance from such evil odours.

Note that it does not matter whether the person in question is your wife/husband or not. Inasmuch as there is a spirit husband/wife in his or her life and you have had sexual intercourse with him/her, your progress in life will be hindered because these invisible demonic robbers called incubus/succubus are regular transporters of demonic particle, which they pollute their victims with.

5. Barrenness or unfruitfulness:

Whenever a spirit husband or wife has sexual intercourse with its victim in the dream, demonic particles are injected into the body of such victim. These unseen particles serve as impediment to child conception and fruitfulness in marriage. These particles can also transform into demonic tumour, fibroid or a swelling of certain part of the reproductive organs and so on.

6. Spirit husbands and wives are the brains behind disagreement and divorce in marriages:

Spirit husbands and wives are the brains behind several divorces witnessed in our society today. They do this with the aim of keeping their victims permanently married or attached to them. They can instil demonic thoughts that can breed baseless quarrel or unnecessary dispute in their victim's marital life. Spirit husband and wife are the brain behind pride in marriage (woman showing pride to her husband and vice versa), frustration, lustful desire, jealousy, covetousness and impatience among couples, and these things have broken several marital unions.

7. Late marriage: Because spiritual husbands and wives are extremely jealous over their victims, they can hinder their victims from having a husband or wife here in the real world. And if at all their victim by divine intervention gets a good husband or wife, they will do everything within their power to frustrate their victim's marital life. For example, they can send hardship, failure, spirit of seduction, lust, etc., their rival's way to make them miserable. They are also the ones behind wrong marriages. They can make their victims to get married to the wrong man or woman, especially one who is also a captive to them, so that they can always have an easy access into both lives. I know of a sister who testified that before her church wedding, her spirit husband appeared to her, telling her not to get married to the husband that God destined her to marry here in the physical world. Sometimes the spirit husband or wife appears in the physical world, to be seen only by their victims. They are responsible for spiritual blindness among those who are seeking for a divinely ordained husband or wife but cannot get.

8. Miscarriage, deformed or polluted children: If a pregnant woman has sexual intercourse in the dream with a spirit wife or husband, it can lead to abortion and the birth of a polluted or a deformed child. This is because the baby's organs can be easily tampered with during such demonic sexual act in the dream, which may eventually lead to deformity or the death of the baby.

9. Spiritual and physical paralysis: Spirit husbands and wives are mostly responsible for the serious spiritual and physical paralyses usually experienced by their victim's husbands or wife's. They can attack to frustrate their victim's husbands or wife's health, businesses or ministry progress in order to simply show their resentment and jealousy.

10. Evil transfer of demonic traits or habit: Satan usually equips his demons succubus/incubus spirit otherwise known as husband/wife with demonic particles that are later transformed into evil traits or habits immediately they access their victims. These habits include

A. Anger

B. Hatred

C. All forms of lust, including sexual and material lust

D. Brain dullness, weakness and procrastination

E. Worldliness and hatred for the things of God

F. Smoking cigarettes or drinking alcohol in order to ward off stress or depression

G. Depression

H. Memory loss

If any of these traits is operative in a life, spirit husbands and wives are the major cause. If you see a man or woman who is always lustful, nagging or quarrelling, such man or woman may have been having sexual intercourse with a spirit husband in the dream.

11. Loss of personal virtue, values and potential: During sexual act in the dream with a spirit husband or wife, certain virtue or potential necessary for progress in life is transferred or given in exchange for the pleasure received. The devil will inject his virtues and extract Godly virtues from you. It does not matter whether you are conscious of it or not; if anything is linking you to a spirit husband or wife and that thing is not destroyed or broken, the spirit husband or wife will continue to have sexual relationship with you in dreams, stealing your potential and strength needed for life exploit. That is why if you ask some people if they know what they are here on earth to do, they will simply tell you, "Well I don't know. I am just living like everyone else". The spirit husband or wife may have robbed them of their potential and ability to reason for success.

12. Eternal destruction in hell: Those who have spiritual husband/wife and are doing nothing to stop the experience will be very surprised if after death they do not make it to heaven. Having sexual relationship with a spirit being is an unconscious sin and an evil union with an unclean spirit. You cannot be having evil fellowship with demonic beings in the dream and at the same time hope to serve God wholeheartedly. Demonic deposit will be operational in your life and will be pushing you into committing sins in the physical world. And because, according to God's word, your whole body, spirit and soul must be preserved blameless unto the coming of the Lord, you need to violently fight this demon that appears in your dreams to give you demonic sexual satisfaction, so that you can be free from the plague of God's judgment that is meant for Satan and all those who are in fellowship with him either physically or spiritually.

If you know you are already a child of God (I mean if you have given your life to Jesus Christ), I want you to rise up right now and pray these prayers with holy violence in your heart against the spiritual husband or wife molesting your life through dreams. Meanwhile, if you have not yet given your life to Jesus Christ, continue to the next chapter of this book, which is Chapter Four, and afterward come back and pray these prayers:

1. Embargos placed upon my household by any demonic spirit or

DELIVERANCE FROM BONDAGE OF THE SPIRIT HUSBANDS AND WIVES

agent, break, in the name of Jesus.

2. Anti-prosperity perfume injected into my life by a spirit husband/wife in the dream, be neutralized by the blood of Jesus.

3. Demonic arrows of rejection and hatred fired into my life by spiritual husband/wife, backfire to your sender, in the name of Jesus.

4. Troublers of my womb, the God of Elijah shall trouble you, in the name of Jesus.

5. Troublers of my greatness, the God that troubled Egypt and Pharaoh shall trouble you, in the name of Jesus.

6. I bind any strongman delegated

against my goodness, in the name of Jesus.

7. Violently and forcefully, I recover all my goodness that has been stolen by any strongman delegated against my life by Satan, in the name of Jesus.

8. By the power of resurrection of our Lord Jesus Christ, I command all my dead potentials and gifts to resurrect now, in the name of Jesus.

9. My finances, receive divine deliverance in the name of Jesus.

10. My businesses, expand by fire and prosper in the name of Jesus.

CHAPTER FOUR

HOW DOES A SPIRIT HUSBAND OR WIFE ACCESS THEIR VICTIM'S LIFE?

You may be asking, how do these demonic spirits known as incubus (spiritual husband) and succubus (spiritual wife) access the lives of their victims? I am going to vividly explain the various doors through which these demons are gaining access into several people's lives on earth.

1. The door of Adamic sin: The sin committed by the first man, Adam, opens the door to oppressions from the satanic world, this including the influence of the spirit husband and wife. Because man lost his ability to have absolute control of his spirit nature to sin (including the ability to control the spirit or unseen world around him), Satan and the fallen angels, otherwise known as demonic beings took advantage of this gap to access and dominate mankind. When Adam yielded himself to sin, he automatically became a servant of sin and according to God's word, wherever sin dwells, there will Satan dominate.

Know ye not, that to whom ye yield yourselves servant to obey, his servants are ye to whom ye obey;

whether of sin unto death, or of obedience unto righteousness? (Romans 6:16)

For the wages of sin is death; but the gift of God is eternal life through Jesus Christ our Lord (Romans 6:23)

The violation of God's commandment by Adam and Eve (his wife) brought all their offspring under the influence of satanic attacks and manipulations. Thank God for the price for sin paid by Jesus Christ at Calvary. Until a man believes and accepts this great price of redemption paid by our Lord Jesus Christ on the cross of Calvary, he cannot have the spiritual power or grace to overcome satanic agents like spirit husbands and wives.

If you have not given your life to Jesus, you need to do so now, so as to be able to receive the power to overcome every negative power of the devil, including spirit husbands and wives.

But as many as received him, to them gave he power to become the sons of God, even to them that believe on his name. Which were born, not of blood, nor of the will of the flesh, nor of the will of man, but of God. (John 1:12-13)

As long as a person is not born again or saved by the saving power of our Lord Jesus Christ, such a person is tagged in the word of God as the son or daughter of Satan. This of course will permit easy satanic access into every facet of such person's life. Satan will also choose a spirit husband or wife whom he will delegate to extract some spiritual substances needed for life's progress from such person, thereby making life unbearable for them.

If you want to have power over spirit husbands and wives and be able to pray the prayer points that will be given at the end of this book, then follow the steps below. It is as simple as ABC.

A= Accept Jesus into your life as your Saviour and be determined to withdraw from your old life of sin into a new life of holiness in Jesus Christ. (Acts 2:37-39)

B= Believe that Jesus died on the cross of Calvary to save you from all your sins, including the one committed by Adam, the first man. (Acts 17:31)

C= Confess with your mouth that Jesus is your Lord and Saviour. (Romans 10:10-13; Acts 2:21)

Say this prayer:

Lord Jesus, I believe you died on the cross of Calvary for my sin. I accept you as my Lord and Saviour today: come into my life and make me your own. From this day, I renounce sin and Satan to follow you, the true and living God. Thank you Jesus for saving me.

If you have sincerely prayed this prayer and you are ready to abandon your old life of sin, then you are qualified to exercise authority through prayers over spirit husband/wife and all other demonic forces terrorizing your wellbeing.

2. The doors of evil or demonic covenants: A covenant is simply a commitment, a bargain or an agreement to a course between two or more people for the purpose of some mutual benefits with conditions binding on the parties in the commitment. Covenants will usually take place between two parties; it may be between a person and another person, a group of persons or family and another group of persons or family, a community and another community, a nation and another nation, or a human and a spirit being. Some covenants are established through the shedding of blood, that is, an animal is slaughtered and the blood sprinkled on the floor to establish the existence of the covenant. This implies that any activity involving the use of animal or human blood for sacrifice either consciously or unconsciously establishes a covenant. A covenant can also be made verbally or through actions i.e. through the swearing of oaths. It is however important to note that even though there are evil covenants, there are also good covenants. The good covenants are the covenants between God and man, sealed by the blood of the lamb (Jesus Christ). As a matter of fact, the entire Holy Bible is a covenant book expressing God's position, will and promises, with conditions for their benefits. Therefore, whenever there is a violation of those promises in the word of God, we can simply conclude that there is a breach in contract or covenant: the only thing that can keep the promise of God effective in the life of the redeemed is their obeying or keeping their part of the covenant or the word of God.

Demonic or evil covenants are not

the same as God's covenant. As a matter of fact, God forbids demonic covenants. They are agreements made by men with Satan or his evil agents or demons, either consciously or unconsciously, which allow Satan or his demons to have access and build a stronghold of evil control over the lives of those in such covenant and those of their offspring. While God's covenant is established by God himself for the betterment of mankind, evil covenants exist to put those in such covenants into serious demonic bondage here on earth and, at the end, earn them eternity in hell. It is an agreement that totally contradicts the will of God. It is through some of these evil covenants that doors are open to spirit husbands or wives to molest men and women. Here are some examples of the evil covenants that can open the door of a person's life to the oppression of spirit husbands or wives.

a. Ancestral evil covenants:

Ancestral evil covenants are those covenants or agreements that were made between one's late or living grandparents with the devil or his demons in the past, and which permit evil access or invasion into the lives of their descendants. Those who have or have had grandparents who have pledged allegiance to some secret idols or evil altars are indirectly under evil ancestral covenant without knowing. Even if you are a Christian, as long as your ancestral parent participated in idolatry in the past, until you break the entire covenant linking you with your ancestral parent's idolatry, the influence of the spirit husband or wife will be very strong over your life. God forbids any relationship with Satan or his demons, which is why he has decided to allow the one who commits idolatry to be punished even unto his or her fourth generation. And if the children of the fourth generation do not confess or break the alliance or covenant with the evil idols, they will also pass the judgment to other generations, thereby allowing Satan and his demons to influence their descendants even though they are ignorant of their ancestral parents' idolatry.

And God spake all these word saying,

I am the LORD thy God, which have brought thee out of the land of Egypt, out of the house of bondage.

Thou shall have no other gods before me.

Thou shalt not make unto thee any graven image, or any likeness of any thing that is in heaven above, or that is in the earth beneath, or that is in the water under the earth:

Thou shalt not bow down thyself to

them: nor serve them: for I the LORD thy God am a jealous God, visiting the iniquity of the father upon the third and fourth generation of them that hate me and shewing mercy unto thousands of them that love me, and keep my commandments. (Exodus 20:1-6)

When you forsake all sins, break every evil covenant and rededicate your life afresh to Jesus, God will become your father, husband, wife, counsellor and guardian. But if you or any of your grandparents is living in sins, especially the sin of idolatry (for instance, the worship of a saint, a deity, wood or a tree, a stone, or any form of carved images, either of gold or of silver), Satan automatically becomes your husband, wife, father, instructor, etc., and as his slave, he can do whatever he desires with you and your descendants. Many grandparents or great grandparents, because of their lust for wealth, prestige and long life, had in the past gone to seek help from Satan inside evil shrines, demonic streams or altars, etc. Some have mortgaged the future of their yet unborn children to Satan. They have given their whole generation to Satan in exchange for their own protection and other selfish desires. So when their children, who are ignorant of these evil commitments made by their forefathers, begin to face demonic oppressions, they will be saying "It is the enemies at work". Some people's state of poverty, lack and demonic oppression today, if properly diagnosed through the fire of prayer, can be traced to covenants that their ancestors made on some ancient evil altar, trading their entire life progress to Satan in exchange for a good harvest of cocoa or kola nut. Evil ancestral covenant permits Satan to have easy access into the lives of the descendants or offspring of those who are into such covenants. Any time there is an opportunity for advancement, Satan will delegate his demons as spirit husbands or wives to go and have sexual intercourse with their victim's descendants so that potential or ability for exploit in life can be stolen from them. While praying for breakthrough in ministry, the Lord immediately instructed me to move to my land of nativity and break evil covenants and strongholds. As soon as I commenced prayer in my home town, strange things began to happen. A member of the family suddenly dreamt of himself and others being loose from a kind of chain. The secret of where the entire family's glory was tied was also revealed. Those Christians having sexual experience with a strange being in their dream should wake up and find out the hidden secret about their family history. Their forefather or ancestors may have covenanted them to a deity or idol in the past, while some might have even been given out as husband or wife to this idol that is now attacking them as a spirit husband/wife to collect their blood for covenant renewal.

b. Self-inflicted evil covenant: Self-inflicted covenants are those agreements made by oneself, either consciously or unconsciously, with Satan or his demonic agents. When a man or woman, because of lack or certain hardship, turns to a native doctor or a witchdoctor for help, he is in reality seeking the help from Satan. Considering the ministry of Satan as a thief, a killer and a destroyer, Satan will begin to steal the future of such person and that of their offspring. Satan has nothing good to offer to anybody. He cannot give you anything without taking something from you in return. His blessings are counterfeit; they will not only fade away with time, but they will also bring a lot of evil consequences on you and your offspring if you turn to him for help. When a person turns to a witchdoctor for help, such a person is automatically in covenant with the devil. And with the existence of such covenant between such person and Satan, Satan will begin to freely access his or her life, either spiritually or physically, as a spirit wife or husband to steal from the person through sexual act in the dream.

c. Sexually acquired evil covenants: Sexually acquired covenants are those covenants that came into a person's life through either his or her past or present unholy sexual relationship. Every unholy sexual relationship has its origin from the queen of heaven, a strong principality working in association with other demonic agents on earth, i.e. seducing and immoral demons. When you have sexual relationship with a man or woman that you are not legally married to or when you sneak out of your matrimonial home to have sexual intercourse with someone else, you are having unholy sexual relationship. By this you are making a strong evil covenant with the demons that originated that unholy sexual act that you are committing. In reality, those who commit unholy sexual act (that is having sexual relationship with people they are not legally married to) are having sexual intercourse with the evil spirits or demons behind such acts. During ejaculation, the semen that goes into the opposite sex is spiritually transferred into the bosom of the demons behind such illicit acts to be used to establish a covenant so that the future of that person involved can be miserable. Automatically, the demons behind such act will eventually become the spiritual husband or wife to the person, appearing in their dream as dream criminals to have sexual intercourse with them or feed them with demonic poisons so as to collect their virtue and steal their destined greatness. A sister who was once a victim of a spirit husband during interrogations declared that her experience with a spirit husband began after she had her first sexual relationship with a man she was not legally married to. If you join yourself to Satan through immoral sins, you will become a slave to Satan and sin. If you know you have given your life to Jesus Christ and you are still committing immoral sins, you need to understand that you have opened the door of your life to the various consequences of the attack of spirit husband or wife. You will therefore need to ask for God's forgiveness and aggressively pray the various prayer points inspired by the Holy Spirit in this book in order to set yourself loose from the bondage of sexual demons like spirit husband/wife.

3. The door of evil dedication: Another door through which spirit husbands or wives can access a person's life is the door of evil dedication. Evil dedications take place when a person is dedicated to a deity or an idol (e.g. queen of the coast, otherwise known as the water spirit; Ogun known as the god of iron in Nigeria; Buddha in the India nation; Apollo the Greek god of music, etc.) either at birth or in adulthood. Evil dedication of children and adults is very rampant in many African and Asian countries because of their numerous idol worshipping. In most cases, animals are slaughtered and their blood placed on the altar or by the riverside for these deities to drink, so that according to the worshippers' own beliefs, the deity will bring blessings and also help them to monitor and protect them and their babies. When the Lord wanted me to move to the southern part of Senegal (West Africa), in the course of prayers, I saw a man standing in the forest and lifting up a little baby to the sun. During that revelation, the Lord said to me, "My son, can you see what they are doing in the dark, dedicating my creature to the gods of the sun?" Arriving in that part of the country, after days of unceasing prayers and revelation, I discovered that the land was filled with all kind of idolatry, fetishism and masquerade spirit worship. The land and the people have been dedicated to the worship of Satan without the inhabitants knowing it. Evil dedication can also take place when couples, because of their inability to have children, run toward demonic agents like witchdoctors or satanic priests to seek for a child. When children acquired from Satan are given birth to, the demons that gave the approval to the birth of those children will put them under serious surveillance, monitoring their growth and progress in life. The same is also applicable to children consecrated to a deity or idol immediately after birth; Satan will make sure their progress is monitored by his demons. If at all those children as adults become born again while still ignorant of the covenant of the evil dedication made by their parents on their behalf, the demons behind those evil covenants of evil dedication will continue to have evil sexual relationship with the children in dreams; manifesting as spiritual husband or spiritual wife in order to strengthen the covenant of evil dedication already in existence and bring evil consequences.

4. Exposure to immoral acts:

Indulging in immoral activities is one of the easiest ways by which a spiritual wife or husband can gain access into any life. For instance, if a man or a woman masturbates or derives pleasure in reading or watching immoral materials such as pornographies, sexually perverted movies, series or novella, such man or woman is simply consenting to a relationship with sexual demons or demons of sexual immorality and lust. By doing that, an agreement or a covenant automatically takes place between them and the demons that originated the production of such pornography materials. From there, a door will be opened for demonic access. These forces of darkness responsible for the printing and making of such pornography materials and movies will began to access his or her life to have sexual intercourse with him or her in the dream. I want you to understand that Satan is the one behind every pornographic publication and movie. His aim is to make sure that people who read or watch pornographic materials are trapped into a covenant with him so that he can control them both physically and spiritually. Those who are addicted to watching nude materials are in bondage to

DELIVERANCE FROM BONDAGE OF THE SPIRIT HUSBANDS AND WIVES

Satan and his demonic spirits already. These people are also the most vulnerable to attack by spirit husbands or wives. Even if you say "I watch pornography with my wife or husband", I want to make it clear to you today that it does not matter whom you are watching it with; it is a serious sin before God. The person whose nakedness you are watching to derive sexual satisfaction or pleasure is not your husband or wife, but a man or woman possessed and disoriented by a demonic spirit and now being used as a tool to pollute other humans and initiate them into a perverted way of living. If you truly want to be free from sexual demons, you must make sure you get rid of all those pornographic pictures and videos on your computer or your phone and burn off all the nude magazines that you keep under your bed, inside your wardrobe or locker in the office. Don't throw them away, as others can access them too; rather destroy them by burning. God's word says that he that is joined to a harlot is one flesh with her, and he that is joined to the Lord becomes one flesh with the Lord (1 Corinthians 6:16). If you join yourself to Satan through immoral acts, he will practically take his abode in you and constantly attack your physical and spiritual life through the operations or activities of spirit husbands and wives.

5. The operation of the queen of heaven: Captives of the queen of heaven are also easy victims of spiritual husband and wife. You may ask, who is the queen of heaven again? The queen of heaven is a strong principality that is specially attached to Satan. She coordinates every satanic operation in human life here on earth (water, land and air). She is responsible for any type of wickedness you can think of here on earth. She has authority to disperse demons at will and obstruct goodly activities on earth. As a matter of fact, as the Holy Spirit is to the saints, so is the queen of heaven to all her captives here on earth. Anyone who obeys and carries out any of her activities here on earth automatically becomes her captive and she can molest them at will with the attack of spiritual husband or wife. Anyone who engages in any of the evil acts below is already a captive of the queen of heaven without knowing:

a. Theft (all kinds of theft)

b. Sexual perversion such as masturbation, fornication, pornography, lesbianism/homosexuality, bestiality, and incest.

c. Adultery

d. Lying

e. Extortion

f.   Prostitution, either partial or fulltime

g.   Witchcraft

h.   Drunkenness

i.   Disobedience to God

j.   Murder

k.   All sorts of rebellion

l.   Occultism

m.   Disobedience to parents — both spiritual parents and biological parents

n.   Hatred

o.   Envy

p.   Jealousy

q. Gossip

r. Idolatry and ancestral worship

s. Ritual practices

As our Lord Jesus is the general overseer of the church on earth and in heaven, the queen of heaven is the delegated principality that oversees the affairs of Satan on earth. She controls the sexual demons known as incubus and succubus (spiritual husband and wife) and can send them to molest her captives who engage in any of the wicked practices named above at will.

The bible talk of the queen of heaven in the book of Jeremiah 7:16-20

"Therefore do not pray for this

people, nor lift up a cry or prayer for them, nor make intercession to Me; for I will not hear you. Do you not see what they do in the cities of Judah and in the streets of Jerusalem? The children gather wood, the fathers kindle the fire, and the women knead dough, to make cakes for the queen of heaven; and they pour out drink offerings to other gods, that they may provoke Me to anger. Do they provoke Me to anger?" says the LORD. "Do they not provoke themselves, to the shame of their own faces?" Therefore thus says the Lord GOD: "Behold, My anger and My fury will be poured out on this place—on man and on beast, on the trees of the field and on the fruit of the ground. And it will burn and not be quenched."

The bible also talk about the Queen of Heaven in Jeremiah 44:17-25

"But we will certainly do whatever has gone out of our own mouth, to burn incense to the queen of heaven and pour out drink offerings to her, as we have done, we and our fathers, our kings and our princes, in the cities of Judah and in the streets of Jerusalem. For then we had plenty of food, were well-off, and saw no trouble. But since we stopped burning incense to the queen of heaven and pouring out drink offerings to her, we have lacked everything and have been consumed

DELIVERANCE FROM BONDAGE OF THE SPIRIT HUSBANDS AND WIVES

by the sword and by famine." The women also said, "And when we burned incense to the queen of heaven and poured out drink offerings to her, did we make cakes for her, to worship her, and pour out drink offerings to her without our husbands' permission?" Then Jeremiah spoke to all the people—the men, the women, and all the people who had given him that answer—saying: "The incense that you burned in the cities of Judah and in the streets of Jerusalem, you and your fathers, your kings and your princes, and the people of the land, did not the LORD remember them, and did it not come into His mind? So the LORD could no longer bear it, because of the evil of your doings and because of the abominations which you committed. Therefore your land is a desolation, an astonishment, a curse, and without an inhabitant, as it is this day. Because you have burned incense and because you have sinned against the LORD, and have not obeyed the voice of the LORD or walked in His law, in His statutes or in His testimonies, therefore this calamity has happened to you, as at this day." Moreover Jeremiah said to all the people and to all the women, "Hear the word of the LORD, all Judah who are in the land of Egypt! Thus says the LORD of hosts, the God of Israel, saying: 'You and your wives have spoken with your mouths and fulfilled with your hands, saying, "We will surely keep our vows that we have made, to burn incense to the queen of heaven and pour out drink offerings to her." You will surely keep your vows and perform your vows!'

Please, if you are involved in any of the wicked acts mentioned above, you are already a captive of the queen of heaven. Jesus called the Pharisees and Sadducees of his days "evil" simply because they were doing the will of their master, the devil. If you do the will of the queen of heaven, you are doing the will of the devil, and she can send her demons as spiritual husband or wife to molest you regularly through sexual intercourse and make you suffer the various consequences of having a spiritual husband or wife.

6. Living in a haunted or polluted house. If a building or house is owned or had once been inhabited or owned by an herbalist or an idol worshiper, such house will become a polluted house that can open access to attack from demonic spirits like spirit wife or husband. Any house constructed through ritual money is also an extension of satanic kingdom here on earth. Those who rent such kinds of houses will find themselves incurring serious loss of virtue and blessing. Spiritual husband or wife will also be visiting them regularly in the dream in order to have sexual intercourse with them, so as to rob them of their virtue and use their blood to renew the covenant made with the true owner of the house. Therefore, those who just move into apartments without prayerfully seeking God's face should beware of falling into the trap of destiny criminals who build houses purposely to lure tenants into evil covenants. So many people have rented polluted houses and instead of progress, it is calamity upon calamity that has invaded their lives; loss of money, bad luck, oppression from demonic spirits, chronic hardship, marital disharmony, and demonic attacks on children and from spiritual husband/wife has been their lot. A lady in France once gave an account of her own experience after watching my online video on the phenomenon of spiritual husband/wife, in French language. She said that since she moved into the apartment where she lives, she has been having very strange experience such as loss of job and dream attack from a spiritual husband that is using different faces to harass her sexually in the dream. Her neighbours, after hearing her story, advised her to quit the house as her experience was not new to them. According to them, the former occupant of the house before she moved in had similar experience.

DELIVERANCE FROM BONDAGE OF THE SPIRIT HUSBANDS AND WIVES

After much enquiry, she later found out that some family who came from Africa and were worshiping voudou (a marine spirit) once lived in that apartment, and through their numerous evil sacrifices and fetishism, they have transformed the apartment to the embassy of Satan. They left the house but they did not go with all their demons. They left those demons there to harass any person who moves into that apartment. Spirit husbands/wives work for Satan. They are one of the strongest tools being used by Satan to renew evil covenant and rob people of their virtue (ability for exploit). If there is a demonic covenant linking your house with

Satan, you need to discover and break it so that Satan will not have any hold over your life's progress.

7. Ungodly dresses: As a Christian, you are not to wear dresses that can attract sexual demons into your life. Those who do not understand should know right now that sexual demons are invisible and they are attracted to anyone who wears indecent dresses.

a.   Ladies wearing trousers with their buttocks outlined for the public to see are carrying immoral demons around without knowing.

b.   Dresses that expose part of your breasts as women can also attract the demon of lusts.

c.   Lipsticks and hair attachments used for seduction are all properties of Satan, and anyone who uses them will attract his demons, including spiritual husband or wife into their life, who will then begin to molest them sexually in dreams.

8. Fetishes on the body and satanic objects in the house: All those who attach fetishes to their bodies, or those who have satanic objects in their homes (either buried or hung in the house) are under the influence of water spirits (demons that live and manipulate their victims from under the sea). Also, satanic objects obtained from witchdoctors or sorcerers, or inherited from parents or great grandparents, can attract spirit husband or spirit wife, who will begin to threaten or harass you in dreams in order to strengthen the covenant attached to those objects.

9. Satanic images or tattoos on the body: Another thing that can expose a person to the attacks of spirit husband or spirit wife is pictures or tattoos engraved on the body. There are those who engrave images of naked women or men, snakes, turtles, lions, and other strange animals on their bodies without thinking of the spiritual implications. There are demonic spirits behind these satanic images or tattoos, and they attract sexual serpent or demons who will begin to harass you in the night while you sleep.

DELIVERANCE FROM BONDAGE OF THE SPIRIT HUSBANDS AND WIVES

If you know that you are already born again and washed with the blood of the crucified lamb Jesus Christ, pray this prayer with all your heart.

1. O Lord, send your divine fire into the foundation of my life and destroy every evil plantation in it, in the name of Jesus.

2. Blood of Jesus, separate me from every demonic covenant plaguing my destiny in the name of Jesus.

3. By fire, by thunder, I cancel and break every relationship between me and Satan, in the name of Jesus.

4. Every stronghold of familiar spirit in my life, break by fire, in the name

of Jesus.

5. Power to excel over demonic obstacles, fall upon me today, in the name of Jesus.

6. Anointing of an overcomer, overshadow me today, in the mighty name of Jesus Christ.

CHAPTER FIVE

STEPS TO DEALING WITH THE SPIRIT HUSBAND AND WIFE PHENOMENON

The spirit husband or wife, like any other demonic spirit, can be dealt with provided you follow the basic steps of dealing with them highlighted in this book.

1. You must be genuinely born again.

The power and the grace to exercise authority over Satan and his demons are only accessible at the new birth. This implies that you need to give your life to God by confessing the Lord Jesus Christ as your Lord and Savior. We said earlier in the second chapter of this book that one of the things that can permit easy access of spirit husband or wife into any life is Adamic sin; that is, the sin committed by Adam and Eve (the first parents of all humans). Adam and Eve committed a grievous sin that made the creator strip them of their authority over Satan. This subjected all mankind to all sorts of satanic oppression, including oppression from spirit wife and husband. In order to be set free from the consequences of the sin committed by Adam, it has therefore become necessary that all mankind, irrespective of their race or colour, be reconciled back to God through the blood of Jesus Christ that was shed on the cross at Calvary.

But God commendeth His love toward us in that, while we were yet sinners, Christ died for us.

Much more then, being now justified by His blood, we shall be saved from wrath through Him.

For if, when we were enemies, we were reconciled to God by the death of His Son, much more, being reconciled, we shall be saved by His life.

And not only that, but we shall also rejoice in God through our Lord

Jesus Christ, by whom we have now received the atonement.

THEREFORE, AS BY ONE MAN SIN ENTERED INTO THE WORLD, AND DEATH BY SIN, SO DEATH PASSED ONTO ALL MEN, FOR ALL HAVE SINNED.

For until the law, sin was in the world, but sin is not imputed when there is no law.

NEVERTHELESS DEATH REIGNED FROM ADAM TO MOSES, EVEN OVER THOSE WHO HAD NOT SINNED IN THE SIMILITUDE OF ADAM'S TRANSGRESSION, HE BEING THE FIGURE OF HIM THAT WAS TO COME.

But not as the offense, so also is the free gift. For if through the offense of one many be dead, much more the grace of God, and the gift by grace, which is by one Man, Jesus Christ, hath abounded unto many.

And not as it was by one who sinned, so is the gift: for the judgment was by one to condemnation, but the free gift is for many offenses unto justification.

For if by one man's offense death reigned by one, much more those who receive abundance of grace and the gift of righteousness shall reign in life by One, Jesus Christ.

Therefore as by the offense of one, judgment to condemnation came upon all men, even so by the righteousness of One, the free gift unto justification of life came upon all men.

For as by one man's disobedience many were made sinners, so by the obedience of One shall many be made righteous.

Moreover the law entered, that the offense might abound. But where sin abounded, grace did much more abound,

that, as sin hath reigned unto death, even so might grace reign through righteousness unto eternal life by Jesus Christ our Lord. (Romans 5:8-21, emphasis added)

But now the righteousness of God without the law is manifested, being witnessed by the law and the prophets;

Even the righteousness of God which is by faith of Jesus Christ unto all and upon all them that believe: for there is no difference:

FOR ALL HAVE SINNED, AND COME SHORT OF THE GLORY OF GOD;

Being justified freely by his grace through the redemption that is in Christ Jesus:

Whom God hath set forth to be a propitiation through faith in his blood, to declare his righteousness for the remission of sins that are past, through the forbearance of God;

To declare, I say, at this time his righteousness: that he might be just, and the justifier of him which believeth in Jesus. (Romans 3:21-26, emphasis added)

Jesus Christ has justified all mankind and made them righteous before God through the blood he shed at Calvary. He also released to all who will confess him as their Lord and Saviour the power to manifest as children of God in dominion over sins and satanic operations.

But as many as received him, to them gave he power to become the sons of God, even to them that believe on his name.

Which were born, not of blood, nor of the will of the flesh, nor of the will of man, but of God (John 1:12-13)

If you want to have power against spirit husband and wife and be able to pray the prayer points that will be given at the end of this book, then follow the steps below. It is as simple as ABC.

A= Accept Jesus into your life as your Saviour and be determined to withdraw from your old life of sin into a new life of holiness in Jesus Christ. (Acts 2:37-39)

B= Believe that Jesus died on the cross of Calvary to save you from all your sins including the one committed by Adam the first man. (Acts 17:31)

C= Confess with your mouth that Jesus is your Lord and Saviour. (Romans 10:10-13; Acts 2:21)

Say this prayer:

Lord Jesus, I believe you died on the cross at Calvary for my sin. I accept you as my Lord and Saviour today. Come into my life and make me your own, from this day. I renounce sin and Satan to follow you, the true and living God. Thank you Jesus for saving me.

If you have sincerely prayed this prayers and you are ready to abandon your old life of sin, then you are qualified to exercise authority through prayers over spirit husbands/wives and all other demonic forces terrorizing your wellbeing.

2. Abstain from worldliness and immoralities.

Withdraw yourself totally from every form of immoral and worldly practice i.e. fornication, adultery, addiction and dependence on pornography materials for sexual stimulation or satisfaction should be totality avoided. If you are presently living with a man or a woman that you are not legally married to, that is fornication. Break such relationship immediately; if not, it will serve as an opening through which a spiritual husband or wife will be accessing your life to molest you sexually and make you suffer the various consequences of having a spirit husband or wife.

Know ye not that your bodies are the members of Christ? Shall I then take the members of Christ and make them the members of a harlot? God forbid!

What? Know ye not that he who is joined to a harlot is one body with her? "For two," saith He, "shall be one flesh."

But he that is joined unto the Lord is one spirit.

DELIVERANCE FROM BONDAGE OF THE SPIRIT HUSBANDS AND WIVES

Flee fornication. Every other sin which a man doeth is outside the body, but he that committeth fornication sinneth against his own body.

What? Know ye not that your body is the temple of the Holy Ghost which is in you and which ye have from God, and that ye are not your own?

For ye are bought with a price. Therefore glorify God in your body and in your spirit, which are God's. (1 Corinthians 6:15-30)

Flee also youthful lusts; but follow righteousness, faith, charity, and peace with those who call on the Lord out of a pure heart. (2 Timothy

2:22)

Love not the world, neither the things that are in the world. If any man love the world, the love of the Father is not in him.

For all that is in the world -- the lust of the flesh, and the lust of the eyes, and the pride of life -- is not of the Father, but is of the world.

And the world passeth away and the lust thereof, but he that doeth the will of God abideth for ever. (1 John 2:15-17)

Fornication, adultery, and sexually perverted or pornography materials must be strictly avoided. Remember, the goal of the spirit husband or wife is to sexually pollute their victims by injecting invisible poison into their bodies so that they can be able to tamper with their potentials, disrupt their marriages, deaden their potentials and render them useless and unproductive in the real world. To withdraw from immorality is to withdrawn from one of the easiest means by which spirit husbands and wives can access any life. If you are the type who loves to watch telenovela you need to stop it, because most of these films are programmed by Satan to initiate a lot of people into lust, immoralities and pollution by spirit husband/wife. Once again, if truly you want to be free from sexual demons, then you must make sure you get rid of all those nude pictures, films or video clips on your computer or your phone and burn off the nude magazines you kept under your bed, inside your wardrobe or in your locker in the office. (Don't simply throw them away as others can thus access them too; rather, burn them). God's word says that he that is joined to a harlot is one flesh with her, and he that is joined to the Lord becomes one flesh with the Lord (1 Corinthians 6:16).

3. Respect the covenant of tithing and offering.

Make sure you are a tither, that is

you pay regularly the 10 percent of your income to God. Spiritual husbands and wives are devourers that look for open doors and error in people's lives to attack.

Will a man rob God? Yet ye have robbed me; but ye say, wherein have we robbed thee? IN TITHES AND OFFERINGS.

YE ARE CURSED WITH A CURSE: FOR YE HAVE ROBBED ME, EVEN THIS WHOLE NATION.

Bring ye all thee tithes into the storehouse that there may be meat in mine house, and prove me now herewith, saith the LORD of hosts if I will not open you the windows of heaven, and pour you out a blessing

(PROSPERITY) that there shall not be room enough to receive it.

And I will rebuke the devourer for your sakes, and he shall not destroy the fruit of your ground, neither shall your vine cast her fruit before the time in the field, saith the LORD of hosts. (Malachi 3:8-11, emphasis added)

Incubus and succubus (spirit husband and wife) are spiritual devourers. If you are not paying your tithes, they will attack you through dreams to diminish your spiritual capabilities so that you will not be able to have sufficient strength to prosper physically: the level of your spiritual strength usually will determine the level of the progress you will make here in the physical world.

4. Break all known and unknown evil covenants: Examine the different kinds of covenants we have discussed in this book and see if there is any that you know you have been involved in, and consciously break such. Make sure you do not have anything to do with idol worshipping again; don't eat food offered to idols as sacrifice or carry their properties with you because they may use them again as an avenue to attack you with the demons of spirit husband and wife. If you have a talisman, evil incense or charm under your roof or in your possession, burn it off. If you are used to joining your family to participate in a traditional idolatry festival, you must stop it now and separate yourself from such practices. If also you have any family member whom you know to regularly visit a witchdoctor, avoid eating from their pot, neither leave your children under their care. Anyone who patronizes a witchdoctor is an extension of satanic artillery; they can poison you or your children in your ignorance, which may of course lead to satanic pollution or control.

Depart ye, depart ye, go ye out from thence, touch no unclean thing; go out of the midst of her; be ye clean, that bear the vessels of the LORD. (Isaiah 52:11)

Towards the end of this book are prayer points that you must compulsorily pray in order to break evil covenants and loose yourself from every power that may be holding you captive to spirit husband or wife.

5. Pray violently against the influence of the spirit husband or wife: You must be ready to violently confront these demonic forces through prayers. Satanic forces require violent resistance before they can be made to flee. Hear what the Bible has to say:

Submit yourselves therefore to God.

Resist the devil, and he will flee from you. (James 4:7)

Be sober, be vigilant, because your adversary the devil walketh about as a roaring lion, seeking whom he may devour.

Resist him, steadfast in the faith, knowing that the same afflictions are accomplished in your brethren who are in the world. (1 Peter 5:8-9)

If you are born again, you are a child of God. You have authority over Satan and all his demons. Our Lord Jesus Christ said,

Behold, I give unto you power to tread on serpents and scorpions and over all the power of the enemy, and nothing shall by any means hurt you. (Luke 10:19)

CHAPTER SIX

PRAYER POINTS TO DEMOLISH SPIRIT HUSBAND/WIFE

The prayer points below should be prayed with fasting for at least three days. They must also be prayed aggressively during the day and through the nights.

Praise and worship for at least 15 minutes before proceeding to the Bible confessions and prayers.

Bible confessions:

I will give you the keys of the kingdom of heaven; whatever you bind on earth will be bound in heaven, and whatever you loose on earth will be loosed in heaven. (Matthew 16:19, NIV)

Shall the prey be taken from the mighty, or the lawful captive delivered?

But thus saith the LORD, Even the captives of the mighty shall be taken away: and the prey of the terrible shall be delivered: for I will contend with him that contendeth with thee, and I will save thy children.

And I will feed them that oppress thee with their own flesh, and they shall be drunken with their blood, as with sweet wine: and all flesh shall know that I the LORD am thy

Saviour and thy Redeemer, the mighty One of Jacob. (Isaiah 49:24-26)

Behold, I give unto you power to tread on serpents and scorpions and over all the power of the enemy, and nothing shall by any means hurt you. (Luke 10:19)

For I will give you a mouth and wisdom, which all your adversaries (including the spirit husband and wife) shall not be able to gainsay nor resist. (Luke 21:15)

Prayer of thanksgiving, confession and cleansing

1.   Heavenly father, I thank you for your great mercy and love towards

DELIVERANCE FROM BONDAGE OF THE SPIRIT HUSBANDS AND WIVES

me.

2. I worship you because you alone are worthy to be praised and honoured.

3. O Lord I exalt you because you alone can answer prayers.

4. I exalt you Lord for your hands are mighty to save and to deliver.

5. Thank you O Lord for sending your only Son Jesus to die for all my sins on the cross of Calvary.

6. Eternal God, look down from heaven and have mercy upon me today, in the name of Jesus.

7. Heavenly father, forgive me all my known and unknown sins, including every immoral act, my

ancestral sins and idol worshipping in the past, in the name of Jesus.

8. Have mercy O Lord and forgive me.

9. Cleanse me wholly with the blood of Jesus Christ, in the name of Jesus.

10. Thank you heavenly father for forgiving me my sins. In Jesus's precious name I have prayed.

Breaking all related covenants (Pray this prayer with holy violence.)

11. I break every evil covenant inflicted upon me by the sins of my father or mother, in the name of Jesus Christ.

12. I break all sexually related

covenants by the power in the blood of Jesus, in the name of Jesus Christ.

13. Every sexually acquired evil covenant from my sexual partners in the past, be broken, in the name of Jesus Christ.

14. I break myself loose from every inherited covenant, in the name of Jesus.

15. Covenant with the evil idol of my father's house, break by the power in the blood of Jesus.

16. Covenant with the evil idol of my mother's house, break by the power in the blood of Jesus.

17. Covenants with the evil idol of my father's house, militating against

my progress, break by fire, break by the thunder of God, in the name of Jesus Christ.

18. I release myself from the cage of the queen of heaven, in the name of Jesus.

19. I release myself from the cage of the leviathan spirit, by the power in the blood of Jesus Christ.

20. I release myself from the cage of the queen of the coast, in the name of Jesus Christ.

21. I release myself from the cage of the marine spirit, by the power in the blood of Jesus.

22. I release myself from the cage of the witches and wizards, in the name

DELIVERANCE FROM BONDAGE OF THE SPIRIT HUSBANDS AND WIVES

of Jesus Christ.

23. Thou forest demon sucking the blood of my destiny, die, die, die, in the name of Jesus Christ.

24. Thou evil power crying against my destiny, die, in the name of Jesus Christ.

25. I receive power to destroy every activity of the spirit husband/wife in my life in the name of Jesus Christ.

26. Every covenant with familiar spirit that is affecting my life, break, by the power in the blood of Jesus.

27. Generational curses influencing my life, be broken today, in the name of Jesus.

28. Every negative plantation in the

foundation of my house, break in the name of Jesus Christ.

29. I loose myself from conscious or unconscious evil covenant by the power in the blood of Jesus.

30. Thou negative powers living in my house, die, die, die, in the name of Jesus.

31. Demon of oppression harassing my finances, drink the blood of Jesus and die, in the name of Jesus Christ.

32. I cancel by the blood of Jesus every evil pronunciation uttered against my life in the dark world, in the name Jesus Christ.

33. Covenant with the spirit husband or wife influencing my life

and destiny, break by God's divine fire, break by God's divine thunder, in the name of Jesus.

34. You demonic spirit manifesting as my husband or wife in the dream, die, in the name of Jesus.

35. I break by the blood of Jesus every covenant between me and every demonic spirit, in the name of Jesus Christ.

36. I divorce spirit husband/wife with the blood of Jesus, in the name of Jesus Christ.

37. Spirit husband/wife, perish out of my life forever, in the name of Jesus.

38. Spirit husband/wife, receive

divine pestilence and be confused, in the name of Jesus.

39. I command the wrath of God to appear as coal of fire and destroy you spirit husband/wife, in the name of Jesus Christ.

40. Spirit husband/wife, receive the arrow of divine affliction right now, in the name of Jesus.

41. I retrieve all my goodness stolen by the spirit husband/wife by the power in the blood of Jesus.

42. I command all the children I have had together with a spirit husband/wife to die and be no more, in the name of Jesus Christ.

43. I put the seal of the blood of

Jesus upon all my children in the physical world, in the name of Jesus.

44. Spiritual husband/wife, I say fall down and die to rise no more, in the name of Jesus.

45. Evil poisons transferred into my blood vessels through any unholy sexual relationship that I have had in the past, come out of my body with all your roots and be roasted by fire, in the name of Jesus.

46. Thou power of invisible poisons terrorizing my life, fall and die, in the name of Jesus.

47. Thou serpentine spirit hidden in any organ of my body, dry off from your root and come out of my

life by fire, in the name of Jesus Christ.

48. You my sex partner in the dream, receive divine coal of fire mingled with horrible tempest and the blood of Jesus, and die, in the name of Jesus Christ.

49. Enemies of my comfort, receive the bread of affliction and die, in the name of Jesus.

50. Every power multiplying afflictions in my life, die by fire, die by thunder, in the name of Jesus Christ.

51. Fire of affliction working against my life, be quenched by the blood of Jesus.

52. Covenant with the marine kingdom, break by fire, break by thunder, in the name of Jesus.

53. Every covenant with the leviathan spirit, break, in the name of Jesus.

54. Every door opened in my life to the attack of spiritual husband/wife, be eternally closed by the power in the blood of Jesus, in the name of Jesus.

55. Satanic embargo placed upon my life and ministry by the demon of spirit husband or wife, be broken by the hammer of God, in the name of Jesus.

56. Marine spirit embargo placed

upon my success, break, in the name of Jesus.

57. Marine spirit embargo placed upon my finances, be broken into pieces, in the name of Jesus.

58. Satanic embargo on my life and ministry, be broken into pieces and be roasted into ashes, in the name of Jesus Christ.

59. I take authority over my dream life in the name of Jesus, and I command all my dreams and visions polluters to die right now, in the name of Jesus Christ.

60. Thou animal of darkness programmed into my dream life, receive divine stone of fire and roast

to ashes, in the name of Jesus.

61. Every evil power sitting on my decision to get married, receive horrible tempest mixed with divine acid and die, in the name of Jesus.

62. Generational curse waging war against my getting married, I cancel you today by the power in the blood of Jesus.

63. Self-inflicted curse waging war against my getting married, I cancel you today, in the name of Jesus Christ.

64. I loose myself from every form of dream pollutions, in the name of Jesus Christ.

65. I vomit every poisonous

substance spiritually injected into my body by any marine agent, by the power in the blood of Jesus.

66. By the power in the blood of Jesus, I loose myself from all satanic dream bondage, in the name of Jesus Christ.

67. I command every sickness transferred into my body through unholy sexual intercourse in the past to be neutralised by the power in the blood of Jesus. (Pray this prayer aggressively.)

68. Inherited family sickness, evaporate from my life right now, by the power in the blood of Jesus.

69. Inherited family curse, break in

my life, in the name of Jesus Christ.

70. Inherited family evil covenants, be broken in my life, in the name of Jesus.

71. Inherited spirit of lust that is presently operating in my life, come out of my life with all your root and die, in the name of Jesus Christ.

72. Demon of sexual perversion that is attacking and molesting my life, receive divine acid mixed with divine shock and be eternally electrocuted, in the name of Jesus Christ.

73. Arrow of evil dedication that is operating in my life, die, in the name of Jesus Christ.

74. Every good thing extracted from my body through sexual intercourse in the dream, be restored now by the power in the blood of Jesus.

75. I separate myself totally from every conscious and unconscious demonic association, in the name of Jesus Christ.

76. Demonic dream serpent that has been assigned against my life, die, in the name of Jesus Christ.

77. You evil animal that is being worshipped in my lineage, die, in the name of Jesus.

78 Power behind my problem, die, in the name of Jesus.

DELIVERANCE FROM BONDAGE OF THE SPIRIT HUSBANDS AND WIVES

79. Arrow of confusion fired into my life by spiritual husband/wife, die, in the name of Jesus Christ.

80. Arrow of infirmities fired into my life, come out of my life with all your root and die, in the name of Jesus Christ.

81. Evil power behind the arrow of confusion fired into my life, receive divine fire and roast to ashes, in the name of Jesus Christ.

82. I refuse to suffer the consequences of the sins of my father in the name of Jesus.

83. I refuse to suffer the consequences of the sins of my mother in the name of Jesus Christ.

84. I refuse to suffer the consequences of the sins of my ancestors, in the name of Jesus Christ.

85. Every strange growth or movement in my body, disappear now by the power in the blood of Jesus.

86. Thou power of dream criminals, be neutralised, in the name of Jesus.

87. Satanic perfume spread over my body by spirit husband/wife, clear away by the blood of Jesus.

88. My brain, receive divine quickening, in the name of Jesus Christ.

89. Evil arrow of failure injected

into my body by spirit husband/wife, come out of my life by fire and be roasted to ashes, in the name of Jesus Christ.

90. Evil arrow of procrastination and laziness injected into my body by spirit husband/wife, come out of my life and roast to ashes, in the name of Jesus Christ.

91. Evil arrow of barrenness injected into my body by spirit husband/wife, come out of my life and roast to ashes, in the name of Jesus Christ.

"Death and life are in the power of the tongue, and they that love it shall eat the fruit thereof". (Proverbs 18:21)

Confess this words of prayers with authority into your life.

92. I confess that I am a child of God, in the name of Jesus Christ.

93. I confess that I am an overcomer through Jesus Christ my Lord, in the name of Jesus.

94. I confess that I am victorious with Christ Jesus.

95. I confess that I am seated in the heavenly places, far above principalities and all the powers of darkness of this world, including spirit husbands/wives, in the name of Jesus.

96. Because I am more than a conqueror, I subdue every activity of

DELIVERANCE FROM BONDAGE OF THE SPIRIT HUSBANDS AND WIVES

Satan, including that of the spirit husband/wife, in the name of Jesus.

97. Blood of Jesus, purge me entirely from every form of impurity, in the name of Jesus Christ.

98. I decree that every yoke and bondage placed upon me by the spirit husband/wife be eternally broken and destroyed, in the name of Jesus Christ.

99. Embargos placed upon my household by any demonic spirit or agent, be broken, in the name of Jesus Christ.

100. Any power chasing away my divine life partner, receive divine furnace of fire and release my true

husband/wife to me in the name of Jesus.

101. O Lord, by your mighty hand of deliverance, deliver me from every embargo placed upon me that is preventing me from getting married, in the name of Jesus.

102. Heavenly father, with your searchlight, locate my divine partner and bring him/her to me, in the name of Jesus.

103. I refuse to marry another person's husband/wife, in Jesus' name.

104. My divinely ordained husband/wife, manifest by fire, manifest by thunder, in the name of

Jesus Christ.

105. My finances, receive divine deliverance, in the name of Jesus Christ.

106. My businesses, prosper by God's divine fire, in the name of Jesus Christ.

107. Terminal diseases operating in my body, be terminated by the fire of God, in the name of Jesus.

108. Anti-prosperity perfume injected into my life in the dream, be neutralised by the blood of Jesus Christ.

109. Demons of anger that have been programmed into my life by spiritual husband or wife, and are now killing

and delaying my divine destiny, die today, in the name of Jesus Christ.

110. Demons of anger that have been programmed into my life right from birth, drink the blood of Jesus and die in the name of Jesus Christ.

111. Demonic arrows of rejection and hatred fired against my life, come out with your entire root and backfire to your senders, in the name of Jesus Christ.

112. Troublers of my womb, the God of Elijah troubles you today, in the name of Jesus Christ.

113. Troublers of my greatness, the God that troubled Egypt and Pharaoh shall trouble you today, in

the name of Jesus Christ.

114. Dead organ in any part of my body, hear the word of the Lord and resurrect by the power in the blood of Jesus Christ.

115. Thou evil arrow of barrenness that was fired against me from the witches' coven, jump out of my body and backfire to your senders, in the name of Jesus Christ.

116. I bind any strongman delegated against my womb, in the name of Jesus Christ.

117. I command all the evil arrows, poisons and enchantments fired against my reproductive organ to come out with all their root right

now and die in the name of Jesus Christ.

118. I bind any strongman delegated against my goodness, in the name of Jesus.

119. I demolish any strongman delegated by Satan against my goodness, in the name of Jesus Christ.

120. Violently and forcefully, I recover all my goodness that has been stolen by any strongman delegated against my life by Satan, in the name of Jesus Christ.

121. By the power of the resurrection of our Lord Jesus Christ, I command all my dead potentials and gifts to

resurrect now, in the name of Jesus Christ.

122. Glory of God, fall upon my life in the name of Jesus Christ.

123. Glory of God, be revealed in my life and family in the name of Jesus.

124. Glory of God, shine forth in my marriage in the name of Jesus Christ.

125. Satanic hindrances to the joy of my marriage, I bury you by the power in the blood of Jesus Christ.

126. Every weapon of the wicked that is targeted at destroying and frustrating my marriage, receive divine stone of fire and perish, in the name of Jesus Christ.

127. Fear, I defeat you by the power

in the blood of Jesus, in the name of Jesus Christ.

128. I command all past sexually transmitted diseases and poisons that are influencing my life to be roasted by fire, in the name of Jesus Christ.

129. I break myself loose from any form of demonic soul-tie to any being, either spiritual or physical, in the name of Jesus Christ.

130. Satanic agents assigned to terminate my life, be terminated in the name of Jesus Christ.

131. Divine doors of prosperity and fulfilment, open unto me today, in the name of Jesus Christ.

132. Failure, I command you to fail woefully in my life and family, in the name of Jesus Christ.

133. Demonic delays, lose your grip over my household and die in the name of Jesus Christ.

134. Every activity of the queen of heaven in my life, catch fire by fire, in the name of Jesus Christ.

135. All that I need to succeed in life that is hidden in the marine kingdom, I recover you right now, by the power in the blood of Jesus. (Speak in tongues for at least 7 minutes.)

136. Holy Ghost fire, enter into the leviathan kingdom and make a great

slaughter on my behalf, in the name of Jesus Christ.

137. Thou queen of the coast, I divorce you today, in the name of Jesus Christ.

138. Thou queen of heaven, I divorce you today, in the name of Jesus Christ.

139. I cover myself with the blood of Jesus, in the name of Jesus Christ.

140. I cover my properties with the blood of Jesus Christ.

141. I cover my household with the blood of Jesus Christ.

142. I cover my reproductive organs with blood of Jesus Christ.

143. I cover my home with the blood of Jesus Christ.

144. I enter into my season of joy in the name of Jesus Christ.

145. I enter into my season of fruitfulness in the name of Jesus Christ.

146. I enter into my season of progress in the name of Jesus.

147. I enter into my season of all-round fulfilment in the name of Jesus Christ.

148. I violently enter into my season of unusual breakthrough in the name of Jesus Christ.

149. Glory of God, fall upon my life in the name of Jesus Christ.

150. Glory of God, be revealed in my life and family in the name of Jesus Christ.

151. Glory of God, shine forth in my marriage in the name of Jesus Christ.

152. Thank you heavenly father for giving me victory over the spirit husband/wife and all its associate demons, in the name of Jesus Christ.

DELIVERANCE FROM BONDAGE OF THE SPIRIT HUSBANDS AND WIVES

ABOUT THE AUTHOR

AUGUSTINE AYODEJI ORIGBO is the president and founder of The Word of His Grace Evangelical Ministry Int'l., a non-denominational Christian organization whose aim is to reach the unreached and disseminate the undiluted message of our Lord Jesus Christ to the dying world through all the godly and peaceable means available. He is a teacher, evangelist and Holy Ghost-trained global intercessor and counsellor of God's word. He is the author of several Christian and deliverance books, including Recovering Your Lost Glory, a book specially inspired by the Holy Spirit to expose and stop the activities of glory robbers in any life.

For prayers and counselling, please call:

002348078166601

Wathapps or call : 00221764958083 OR 002349099991032

Or write to:

Augustine Ayodeji Origbo

The Word of His Grace Evangelical Ministry

B.p 15577 Dk-Fann., Senegal

Mailto: wgeministry@yahoo.fr

austine_71@hotmail.com

DELIVERANCE FROM BONDAGE OF THE SPIRIT HUSBANDS AND WIVES

Made in the USA
Columbia, SC
20 September 2023

23141111R00087